Original title:
A Brooch of Grace

Copyright © 2025 Creative Arts Management OÜ
All rights reserved.

Author: Natalia Harrington
ISBN HARDBACK: 978-1-80586-169-0
ISBN PAPERBACK: 978-1-80586-641-1

Reflections in Glistening Silence

In a shiny little world, where no one seems to care,
A lady lost her charm, she found it in her hair.
With pearls that winked and giggled, like tiny little gnomes,
She strutted past the mirror, while talking to her comb.

A squirrel perched beside her, with a nut beneath his paw,

He wore a jaunty hat, oh what a sight to draw!
Together they confounded, the onlookers nearby,
"Just look at that diploma!" they'd chuckle, passing by.

She jangled all her treasures, a marching band display,
With every little treasure, she'd dance the night away.
The squirrels joined the chorus, in a symphony of cheer,
They all sent goofy messages, to squirrels far and near.

And every time a friend stopped by, to gasp and take a peek,
She'd wink and give a twirl, then inadvertently squeak.
In a world of laughter, with every gem in place,
She claimed her little kingdom, with style and lots of grace.

Crest of Poise

On my lapel, a quirk I wear,
With rhinestones bright, beyond compare.
It winks and nods, a playful tease,
Like squirrels at play among the trees.

Worn with flair, it brings a grin,
A chatty friend, it pulls me in.
Together we dance through a sea of faces,
In laughter's embrace, we find our places.

Fragments of Worn Splendor

Tiny jewels, all askew,
A patchwork heart, a right-on cue.
They jive and clink when I walk by,
Like a comedy show, oh my!

Each piece tells tales of clumsy falls,
Of pasta spills and karaoke calls.
A treasure chest, my outfit's gem,
Turns every blunder to a whim.

Veil of Graceful Remembrance

In the mirror, what do I see?
A sparkle caught, it's laughing at me.
It twirls atop my collar high,
Making me blush, oh my, oh my!

Each reflect brings back moments past,
From childhood dreams to ages vast.
With every glance, I giggle and sigh,
This sparkly veil knows how to fly.

The Delicate Emblem

An emblem perched with a wink so sly,
Caught in the spotlight, watch it pry.
It's a chatterbox upon my chest,
Telling secrets like it knows best.

With petals bright and colors bold,
It spins tall tales, both new and old.
In a world of chaos, it winks and plays,
A delicate jester, bringing up rays.

Echoes of a Radiant Past

Once I wore my grandma's pin,
It sparkled bright, oh, what a grin!
But then it fell, oh what a clatter,
My cat took it, now it's his platter.

In parties, it was quite a sight,
Dancing while it shone so bright.
But every twirl, a game of chance,
I lost the pin in my wild dance.

Adorning Moments of Clarity

I found a gem in the thrift shop,
It looked like food, made my heart stop.
A candy brooch, oh what a tease,
Wore it to dinner, caused a freeze.

Friends laughed hard, they were enthralled,
Thought I was trendy, they all called.
But as I chewed my gum with flair,
The brooch fell off—now that's unfair!

The Charm of Subtle Splendor

With a flower pin in my hair,
I strutted round without a care.
But mid-sentence, it flew like a bird,
Landed in soup, so absurd!

I paid a price for my bright style,
With every bite, a soup-filled smile.
Yet, all the guests, they surely knew,
They wanted one too—what a brew!

Radiant Echoes of Grace

Wore a star pinned on my sleeve,
Thought I'd dazzle, make 'em believe.
But during lunch, it flipped on down,
Hit my pasta—oh, how profound!

Lasagna chunks stuck to the star,
Friends chuckled hard, from near and far.
Next week, I thought, I'd try again,
But with a pin that won't offend!

Elegance Embodied

In a world of chaos and to-do,
An outfit shines bright like morning dew.
A pin on the lapel, it winks with cheer,
Attracting odd stares from those who come near.

With feathers and sparkles, oh what a sight,
It dances in laughter, a comedic delight.
Who knew such style could bring on the giggles?
As it flutters about, everyone wiggles!

Trinket of Serenity

A tiny bauble resting on cloth,
Wearing it brings joy, that's no troth.
It smiles like sunshine, blinks with flair,
Turning grumpy folks into happy air.

As it jigs and wiggles, what a thrill,
Bringing laughter, oh yes, what a skill!
It might seem daft, but oh what a fun,
This trinket persists, like the jest of the sun!

Adornment of Whispers

Whispers of delight in its dainty style,
Gather 'round friends, stay for a while.
With every flutter, it quips a tease,
To wear it takes nerve, but grips you with ease.

It giggles and twirls, oh what a tease,
Making you feel like you're dancing with bees.
A conversation starter, a jest on the side,
With each glance it captures, it sprinkles the pride!

Jewel of Quietude

A jewel so quiet, yet full of glee,
Sitting so still on a cup of tea.
Its charm and its antics, a delightful chore,
Making quiet moments burst into more!

As it hums and bobs, what a quirky flair,
Bringing joy to the room, without a care.
In stillness, it sparkles, in laughter, it plays,
Creating a symphony in the most subtle ways!

Tides of Grace

With waves that dance on sandy shores,
The seagulls laugh and call for more.
A flip-flop stuck in salty foam,
Waves play tricks, nowhere feels like home.

Tides roll in, then slip away,
Like socks that vanish come laundry day.
A beach ball bounces, oh what a sight,
As kids run amok, pure morning delight.

Umbrellas tip and sun hats fly,
A twist of fate, the ice cream's shy.
Sandy toes and giggles abound,
In this clamorous joy, we're heaven-bound.

A Tapestry of Radiance

Bright threads weave through laughter and cheer,
Knitted stories we hold so dear.
A cat in a hat, with a playful glance,
Paws on the yarn, joins in the dance.

Colors clash, yet harmonize too,
Like my attempts at a culinary stew.
With bobbles and loops, the fabric spins,
Frogs in the garden wear silly grins.

A nose that twitches, a stitch that's wrong,
We giggle away all day long.
Wrapped in warmth, laughter's embrace,
Living this life, a comedic chase.

The Soft Gleam of Yesterday

In the mirror, old jokes reflect,
Mom's hairdo fails, a real defect.
With curlers clinging like spies in the night,
Cringe-worthy moments, a true delight.

That ice cream spill on grandma's dress,
We all just laugh, it's pure happiness.
Remember the time the parrot swore?
I swear I saw dad hit the floor!

From silly dances to karaoke screams,
In every photo, we're living the dreams.
With love as our glue and giggles, our aim,
We cherish these moments, forget the shame.

The Elegance of Tender Moments

A tea party set with mismatched cups,
Cakes that lean—oh, what a mix-up!
Sugar spills, laughter fills the air,
As crumbs gather, we haven't a care.

A cat in a bow tie looks quite dapper,
Yet fails to recognize he's quite the happer.
With fancy spoons and silly prattle,
Pretending we're nobles, oh what a battle!

Desserts fall down, and giggles erupt,
Friendship's the theme, perfectly corrupt.
In these moments, we shine and glow,
Elegance dressed in chaos, oh what a show!

A Dance of Beauty and Reverie

In a closet full of flair,
A sparkly clip jumped in the air,
Twisted and twirled with such delight,
Tickling my heart, oh what a sight!

As I pinned it to my coat,
My neighbors thought it was a goat!
Laughing, I twirled around the room,
With a shiny charm to chase the gloom.

Each spin revealed its dazzling sheen,
Like a disco ball, so bright and keen,
It whispered softly, 'Join the fun!'
While I danced like a wobbly bun!

People laughed, a joyful sight,
As my outfit brought pure delight,
With each move, I felt carefree,
Embraced by humor and glee.

The Memory of Light

A tiny pin that's quite absurd,
It glistens like a silly bird,
Perched upon my shirt with grace,
Making me giggle, what a place!

It remembers all the laughs we had,
At moments when I felt so bad,
It sparkles bright, a shining drone,
Making every frown feel overblown.

In the mirror, I see a dance,
Of colors swirling, what a chance!
Reflecting all my quirks and jest,
A beacon calling, 'Life's the best!'

So here's to that pin, so light and free,
Wearing it boldly, just let me be,
For laughter's the memory of delight,
With that little spark of shining light.

Threads of Graceful Serenity

A thread of gold, a pinch of flair,
Tied together without a care,
It hangs upon my robe just right,
Casting giggles in morning light.

With tiny beads that jingle so sweet,
It dances with joy, oh what a feat!
Worn on days that feel quite gray,
This silly charm keeps blues at bay.

Around my neck, it sways and swings,
A quirky game, oh the joy it brings!
Every chuckle wrapped in its glow,
Turns every moment into a show!

In a game of whimsy and glee,
Who knew a thread could make me see,
That humor wrapped in elegance true,
Can lift the heart and bubble anew.

The Essence of Shining Repose

A twinkling jewel with a wink and grin,
Bringing giggles from deep within,
Adorning hats and scarves so neat,
It whispers, 'Come dance with me, sweet!'

On lazy days, it catches the sun,
With a glimmer that says, 'Let's have fun!'
Each shimmer and shine, a playful tease,
Like a cheeky breeze that brings you ease.

Reminding all to stop and smile,
To laugh and live, if just for a while,
Wrapped in warmth, like a cozy hug,
It sparkles brightly, a friendly bug!

So here's to charm in every place,
With laughter woven, a lively lace,
Let the essence of joy reside,
Dance with your sparkles, let them guide!

Token of Reverie

In a world where weird is wise,
A sparkly pin caught my eye.
It danced on my lapel with glee,
A tiny jester making me smile.

It twirled and swayed without a care,
Gossiping secrets in the air.
Was it a butterfly or a bee?
Oh wait, it's a brooch, fancy free!

Every outfit feels like a show,
With this gem, I steal the glow.
A bit of whimsy on my chest,
Who knew style could be such a jest?

With each wiggle, I can see,
This token's bringing all the glee.
It giggles back when I'm in fright,
Making every moment feel just right.

Bauble of Solace

A trinket rests upon my frame,
Bright as the sun, it loves the fame.
It whispers to me, "Let's not be plain,"
Cheering my heart to dance in rain.

From dusty shelves to café tables,
This quirky charm, oh yes, it fables.
With every chuckle, I wear it proud,
In a crowd of giggles, I stand unbowed.

It's not just bling, it's quirky cheer,
A little laugh that draws me near.
On gloomy days, it shines the best,
A smiley face upon my chest.

So here's to my delightful piece,
A funny friend that brings me peace.
Life's serious, but I'll outshine,
With this bauble, I'll be divine!

Essence of Refinement

Oh, elegance wrapped in shiny flair,
This sparkly thing with nary a care.
It grins at me, oh what a tease,
A refined laugh that's sure to please.

Dressed to the nines, I'm quite a sight,
With this shiny friend so bold and bright.
It winks and nods with every move,
Such fancy fun, it's in the groove.

Refinement? Please! It's all in fun,
With laughter leading, we happily run.
Who needs poise when you can jest,
This charming piece, I love it best.

So here we are, a merry pair,
Chasing giggles through the air.
It's not just style, but joy that's found,
With a dash of humor, I'm truly crowned.

Locket of Dreams

Nestled close to my quirky heart,
A locket that plays the silliest part.
Open it up, what will I find?
A dance of dreams that's gently twined.

It sways and jingles as I prance,
Winks at the world, oh what a chance!
A childhood wish in shiny disguise,
With every glance, it hypnotizes.

In this tiny chamber of delight,
Live the dreams I hold so tight.
With a silly grin and a little flair,
My locket of dreams takes to the air.

As I strut through life with style and glee,
This charming piece sings songs to me.
It's not just a jewel, it's a riot,
With each heartbeat, it starts a diet!

Ornament of Tranquility

On the table sits a cat,
Wearing pearls, imagine that!
With a wink and a sly purr,
Claims she's queen without a stir.

Among the cushions, a shoe lies,
Left behind in a world of sighs.
The dog wears it like a crown,
Prancing proudly, never down.

A squirrel stealthily creeps near,
In shades so bright, he shows no fear.
Gathering acorns, throwing flair,
His style's met with quite a stare.

And here I stand, with mismatched socks,
Laughing at the clock's loud ticks and tocks.
In chaos, there's a certain tune,
Life's odd rhythm makes me swoon.

Keepsake of Tenderness

The goldfish wears a tiny hat,
With a poofy tail, imagine that!
He swims around like he's the boss,
In his bowl, he's a dapper gloss.

The rabbit hops with grace and flair,
Donning shades that make folks stare.
His whiskers twitch with every hop,
Spreading joy, he just can't stop.

A parrot squawks a cheeky tune,
Dancing like it's high noon.
With feathers bright, he takes the stage,
His antics sparking quite the rage.

And in the garden, turtles race,
Sporting ties in their slow-paced chase.
They're the stars of a laughable show,
Taking their time, moving slow.

Pendant of Beauty

A rogue snail glides with blingy flair,
Adorning pearls, he doesn't care.
With a shell of decorated might,
He slides along, what a sight!

The butterfly wears a tiny ring,
Flaunting colors that make hearts sing.
She flaps about, a queen so bold,
In her garden, she reigns gold.

A hedgehog in a tutu prances,
In ballet shoes, he takes his chances.
With tiny leaps and graceful spins,
He wins the crowd with silly grins.

A ladybug in glasses reads,
On a leaf, she plants her seeds.
She chuckles at the world afar,
Her tiny heart, a shining star.

Flair of Enchantment

The frog wears a sparkly crown,
Croaking jokes, he won't back down.
In a pond, he reigns as king,
Ribbiting tales with a joyful swing.

A raccoon dons a great big coat,
Filling pockets with what he wrote.
With a smirk and a playful leap,
He steals the stage, and the audience weeps.

A bee with a tiny vest so neat,
Buzzes along, quick on his feet.
With a sense of humor so bright,
He tickles flowers, what a sight!

And there's a snail with a party hat,
Spreading cheer like a friendly brat.
Its spiraled shell, a whimsical dream,
Celebrates life, a joyful theme.

Sculpture of Kindness

In a garden of laughter, they sway,
Funny hats worn the wrong way.
A statue made of gumdrops bright,
Winks at the sun, what a silly sight.

Balloons tied to a chicken's wing,
Chasing after the joy they bring.
Kindness carved in chocolate bars,
Sprouting smiles like candy stars.

Dancing trees with silly shoes,
Telling tales that tickle and amuse.
A sculpture of kindness at play,
Turning frowns to giggles each day.

With every giggle, the world feels light,
In this wacky world, all seems right.
Beneath their laughter, bright and bold,
The secrets of kindness start to unfold.

Sparkling Echoes

In a room where giggles jiggle,
Echoes shimmer and make you wiggle.
A disco ball shaped like a fish,
Reflects the dreams of every wish.

Cakes that dance and pies that sing,
Spinning around like a joyful fling.
Sparkles sprinkled on a silly hat,
Make the room burst in cheerful chitchat.

And whispers of laughter spread like light,
Brightening hearts with sheer delight.
Echoes of humor, soft but clear,
Are the melodies we hold so dear.

With each chuckle, a sparkle blooms,
Creating joy that forever looms.
In a sea of laughter, we find our way,
And dance with echoes of a brighter day.

Heirloom of Meaning

Old wallets full of mismatched bills,
Carry stories and grandma's thrills.
An heirloom quilt, with patches bold,
Holds secrets of love later untold.

Grandpa's shoes that squeak with pride,
Take us on adventures wide.
Each button a badge of stories grand,
Woven with laughter, hand in hand.

A treasure chest with socks that twirl,
Holds the wonders of a giggling girl.
Heirloom of meaning, wrapped in jest,
Tickling hearts, it's simply the best.

Through laughter and joy, we weave our tales,
As love and humor light our trails.
For in the fabric of silly and sweet,
An heirloom of meaning makes life complete.

Whimsy in Stillness

In a quiet nook where silliness hides,
A chair that rocks just for giggling rides.
With pillows shaped like laughing cats,
And teacups that dance with party hats.

A clock that ticks with a funny face,
Time giggles softly, moving with grace.
Crumpets wearing tiny shoes,
Swaying to rhythms of jolly blues.

A tapestry stitched with silly loops,
Holds the laughter of whimsical groups.
In stillness, the joy quietly sings,
Whimsy fluttering like butterfly wings.

Each moment a pause filled with delight,
Awakens the heart on a calm night.
In the hush of the world, let laughter spill,
For whimsy in stillness is the sweetest thrill.

Jewel of Subtlety

Upon her blouse a spark does cling,
A shiny piece, a quirky thing.
It winks and nods in bright sunlight,
A talking gem that takes to flight.

Her friends all giggle, 'What a catch!'
'Is that a brooch or just a scratch?'
It tells a story, oh so bold,
Of coffee spills and secrets told.

She wears it sideways, it's a thrill,
Displaying charms, and lots of will.
A fashion statement, loud and clear,
A snappy laugh, a wink, a cheer.

With each small jingle, all can see,
A jester's crown of pure esprit.
Her subtle art, a daily prank,
In jewels, she swims, she rarely sank.

Embrace of Elegance

A tiny pin upon her dress,
With moody blues, it likes to impress.
As people stare, she does a twirl,
The brooch just rolls, it loves to whirl.

Her shopping bag? A whirlwind spree!
She buys 'one more' with glee, oh me!
Did she just wear that yesterday?
The pin just smiles, come what may.

Friends join in with laughter grand,
'We're making memories, super planned!'
The elegance, a silly game,
That tiny pin, it steals the fame.

With every poke and playful dot,
The charm she wears, it sure is hot.
Dancing through life with styled zest,
That little thing? It is the best!

Blooming Resilience

A flower bright upon her coat,
With petals made from rubber boat.
It blossoms wide, despite the gray,
Who knew a plant could go astray?

It sways with wind, a lively freak,
'Today I'm pink,' it seems to squeak.
A joke between her and the sun,
They play all day, and have such fun.

Daisies laugh when winds collide,
While bees and bugs sit right outside.
With blooming spirit, nothing's drear,
She wears her jewel, grinning ear to ear.

No wilt in sight, it's quite a tease,
With petals bright like summer breeze.
A fragile charm that won't give in,
A funny flower, bold within.

Woven in Stardust

Stars collide to form a pin,
Upon her lapel, a cosmic grin.
'The universe,' the glitter claims,
Yet all it does is play silly games.

It tinkles bright when she moves fast,
A cosmic giggle from the past.
With twinkling flair, it has its way,
A starry joke, come night or day.

Friends joke, 'Is that your inner star?'
'It's brighter than your wish on Mars!'
They share a laugh and twinkling dream,
In stardust jokes, they're all agleam.

To wear the night upon her chest,
A teardrop gem, a starlit jest.
The universe? It's just a play,
In cosmic laughs, they laugh away!

Emblem of Poise

In a pocket, tucked away,
A cat sneezed and flew astray.
With all my cool, I tried to catch,
But ended up with quite a scratch.

The teetering heels, oh what a sight,
Wobbling like a toddler, not quite right.
A graceful swirl turned into a twirl,
I laughed aloud, oh what a whirl!

My coffee cup, a balancing act,
It tipped and spilled, what a distract!
But with a grin, I faced the spill,
That morning dance gave such a thrill!

So here I stand, with charm and flair,
Tripping lightly, without a care.
With every slip, I find my grace,
Together we laugh, in this funny place.

Charm of the Heart

A wink, a smile, a comedic twist,
In every glance, something's amiss.
I wore my heart right on my sleeve,
But tripped on it, I must believe!

With every joke that fell flat,
I charmed the crowd, imagine that!
And when I danced with two left feet,
They clapped for more, not missing a beat!

My buttons pop, my laughter bursts,
Chasing dreams, I quench my thirst.
With every blunder, joy's not far,
I strut along, a true rock star!

The echoes of my silly whims,
Like music playing on a whim.
In funny moments, hearts unite,
Celebrating all, with sheer delight!

Gemstone of Harmony

In a garden, blooms so bright,
I sneezed and startled with delight.
The butterflies took quite the chance,
To join my silly, awkward dance!

A flower crown upon my head,
I pranced around, my face all red.
I waved to bees, they looked quite stunned,
As I spun about, my laughter funned!

The sun was shining, not a care,
In this chaos, we find the rare.
With every giggle, joy takes form,
Like gemstones gleaming, a happy norm.

With friends beside me, hand in hand,
Our harmony turns to comic band!
In silly prances, we take our cue,
Creating humor, like morning dew.

Radiance in Stillness

A statue posed in complete chill,
But then came laughter, what a thrill!
From stone to giggles, what a change,
The serious face turned quite strange!

With puns and quips, I held my place,
In silent joy, I found my grace.
The world around me spun and swayed,
Yet in my heart, the laughter played.

I pulled a pose, struck it like art,
While friends erupted, laughter's part.
With every freeze, the memories gleam,
In radiance found, a joyful theme.

So here's to stillness with a twist,
A chuckle shared, we can't resist.
Embrace the funny, bright with cheer,
In every moment, radiance near!

Kinetic Grace

In a dance of twirls and spins,
My outfit sings, a laugh begins.
With each step, chaos reigns supreme,
Caught in the fabric of a dream.

My shoes, they squeak like playful mice,
While I attempt a leap, so nice.
Down I go, a tumble and roll,
Graceful? Perhaps, but not my goal.

The Symbol of Quiet Dignity

A hat that's tilted, just askew,
Says I'm refined, but what's the view?
With every nod, it flops and sways,
Elegant moments turn to plays.

My pockets bulge like squirrels in fall,
Each crumpled note, they have a call.
It's decorum, I must insist,
Though dignity may just be missed.

Glowing Traces of Time

Time marches on, with shoes so bright,
They catch the sun, a dazzling sight.
But every step squeaks like a door,
Echoing my past, forever more.

With wrinkles here and knickers there,
I strut about without a care.
My wardrobe's ancient — vintage chic,
But the laughter? That's what I seek.

The Adornment of Refreshing Solitude

In silence reigns my favorite dress,
It's soft and comfy, I must confess.
With snacks galore and Netflix too,
This solitude? A perfect view.

A crown of snacks upon my head,
I sit and feast, my heart well-fed.
With laughter rising like the tide,
In my cozy nook, I will abide.

Twinkling Embers of Reflections

In the mirror, I waved at my hair,
It waved back, a feathery affair.
With each brush, a dance, a bit wild,
A trusty companion, my inner child.

A sparkle here, a glimmer there,
My blouse says "fashion"; my socks don't care.
Clashing colors, like a circus parade,
Outfit chaos, but I'm unafraid.

Unexpected laughs, from those nearby,
Whispers of style as time passes by.
Yet in this mess, I see my delight,
Flawless quirkiness sets the mood right.

So here's to the charm of all that's odd,
To treasures in chaos, give a nod.
Shining bright in the mirth of the day,
With twinkling embers, we laugh away.

A Legacy Worn Lightly

Grandma's pearls, slightly askew,
Tell stories of dances, a girl of few.
Each clasp a giggle, each strand a grin,
Of family tales that are tucked within.

Worn on a Tuesday, quite underdressed,
The cat ponders if I'm looking my best.
With mismatched socks and no real plan,
I'm a fashionista, or so I span.

Mom says, "Keep it simple and neat!"
But pattern chaos makes my heart beat.
Legacy heavy, yet light as a feather,
Humor and love, they go together.

So here's to bright laughter wrapped in lace,
To treasures so silly, all out of place.
Each trinket a giggle that grassily sways,
A legacy cherished in comical ways.

The Locket of Quiet Radiance

Nestled in cotton, a locket so old,
Holds secrets of joy, and stories bold.
It swings when I move, a metallic beep,
A chatter of dreams and secrets to keep.

With a twist and a turn, it shimmies about,
Making me wonder, what's that all about?
A peek through the glass, it's such a delight,
Smiles in the past keep my future bright.

It doesn't know fashion, nor time's clever game,
Yet it sparkles with laughter, like sunshine's flame.
Around my neck, it jangles with cheer,
Each moment I wear it, I hold dear.

So here's to the joy in the quirkiest keep,
A charm that shares giggles, hardly discreet.
In the locket's embrace, my heart dances free,
In radiant whispers, a laughing decree.

A Poised Adornment

A clip in my hair, oh, what a sight,
It twirls and it sways, dancing at night.
Though grandma insists it's seen better days,
It beams with a confidence that never delays.

My earrings are mismatched, a glorious feat,
Like spices combined in a dish that's a treat.
Each jingle a chuckle, each swing a cheer,
In this playful chaos, I find my frontier.

People may gawk, but I'm in my zone,
A fashion explorer, my spirit's my own.
And with every glance, a laugh is released,
A poised adornment, my joy is increased.

So here's to the silly, the strange, and the fine,
For laughter's a gem that forever will shine.
Let's toast to the quirks, the whims, and the grace,
In this dance of adornments, we find our place.

A Pinch of Poetic Dazzle

In the drawer it hides away,
With glitter lost in yesterday.
A sparkle waits for a grand debut,
To twinkle bright in a sea of blue.

Oh, the tales that it could tell,
Of fashion fails and wishing wells.
Once it danced on a velvet sash,
Now it dreams in a quiet stash.

Stuck on hats of all the quirks,
Promoting smiles, not just perks.
A cowboy hat or a sun-scorched cap,
Its charm can bridge any style gap.

With a pin, it lost its original flair,
But still brings joy everywhere.
So here's to shimmering things we miss,
In our quirky lives, let's reminisce!

Elegy for a Lost Ornament

Oh, my gem, where did you flee?
Under couch cushions, or stuck in a tree?
You once were mighty, fierce, aglow,
Now you're a mystery, where did you go?

Was it a thief with a crafty plan,
Who saw your shine and then ran?
Or did you roll off during a dance,
Escaping the crowd, not giving a chance?

In a pocket or under a toy,
You brought me moments of pure joy.
I'll mourn your sparkle, my once dear friend,
Til I find you again, or at least, pretend!

But life goes on, with or without,
I'll keep designing, that's what it's about.
For every loss brings another chance,
To twirl in style, and to laugh and prance!

Glimmers of Timeless Beauty

A shimmer caught in ribbons tight,
Twinkling whispers, oh, what a sight!
It once adorned a dress so grand,
Now a cat toy in the silly band.

Adorned with stickers and glitter galore,
It simply cannot take anymore.
But in the chaos, it shines so bright,
Making even mismatched socks feel right!

Nostalgia drips with every glance,
As I wear it proudly for a silly dance.
With every wobble, a laugh erupts,
In the treasure chest of life, it's not corrupt!

So here's to all the strange treasures we own,
Reflecting glimmers of beauty shown.
Each quirky piece tells a tale anew,
In this bizarre world, it's me and you!

The Aura of Delicate Adornment

With every clasp, a journey starts,
A colorful tale that jumps and darts.
It sparkles on blouses, pants, and bling,
Singing melodies and joyful zing.

Once pinned on the lapel of my clumsy friend,
Chasing breezes that never quite blend.
The neighbor's cat thought it was food,
Only to witness its radiant mood!

Adornments lost, yet never forget,
Worn by the brave, like a battlefield vet.
In odd places, they find their worth,
Pixelated dreams since the day of birth.

So here's to life's odd little things,
That burst with joy and the laughter it brings.
In pins and patches, we find our grace,
With a wink and a chuckle in this crazy space!

Embers of Refinement

In a crowd of clumsy movers,
I slipped on my sequined shoe,
Did a twirl, became a dancer,
Then tripped on a baby kangaroo.

Classy is my middle name,
But grace just won't cooperate,
I waved like a queen on parade,
And lost my drink to my pearly plate.

Fancy parties look like art,
Until the cake decides to fall,
I'll capsize in swift dismay,
And laugh as crumbs make me small.

So here's to poise and mishap,
A fine blend of fuss and fun,
Life's a dance, a goofy jig,
While laughter sings and troubles run.

Shimmering Threads of Time

Time glimmers like a slippery fish,
I tried to catch it with a net,
But instead, I snagged a napkin,
Which just left me soaked and wet.

With threads of laughter all around,
I tried to spin a tale today,
But ended up wrapped tight in yarn,
And lost my point along the way.

Bling and sparkle, all aglow,
I swirled to show my pretty flair,
Tripped on my own shiny self,
And rolled right into a stranger's hair.

So here's to all our clumsy times,
Where laughter is a worthy prize,
We'll twirl and spin, and miss our marks,
Serene chaos—just the best of skies.

Grace in the Gilded Moment

I strolled in heels made for art,
Expecting to just glide and sway,
But my foot caught a tiny pet,
Now I've got a cat on display!

My dress twinkles like the stars,
As I waltz, I accidentally flash,
My bum's the star of the evening,
While I make a quick and hurried dash.

A swirl of ribbons, colors bright,
With drinks in hand, my dance was grand,
Until I mistook my friend for cake,
And sent frosting on my best mate's hand.

So let's toast to grace on the go,
With giggles and snacks we won't outgrow,
For in these moments slightly wild,
We find our charm, mischievous and styled.

The Charm of Poised Perfection

In a world where grace is chic,
I slipped on ice, oh what a sight,
Did a lovely flop and roll,
With elegance that took flight.

Posed like a statue in the square,
Then a pigeon made its claim,
I laughed as it sat on my head,
Adding flair to my fashion game.

A twinkle in my sip of drink,
I tried to swirl and look so cool,
But dumped it all on my best friend,
Now we're the toast from pool to school!

So here's to poise that laughs and spins,
With goofiness as our perfect touch,
In moments where we lose our grace,
We find our joy and love so much.

Subtlety in Gemstone Whispering

In a hidden nook, a jewel sings,
A little stone with grander things.
It winks and laughs, so sly and bright,
A joke in the pocket, pure delight.

On the lapel, it jostles a bit,
Ooze of charm with every split.
It giggles gently, wears a grin,
"Who wore me first? Just let's begin!"

A twist of fate, connections made,
With each sharp glance, a charade played.
The sparkle shines, with smart retorts,
Witty whispers, the best of sorts.

In gatherings where laughter thrives,
A gemstone jester, full of jives.
Who knew such sparkle could impart,
A sneaky grin upon the heart?

Glorious Hues of Remembered Grace

Ribbons of color weave through air,
Each hue a laugh, just beyond compare.
In sunlight's glow, they twirl and dance,
A vibrant tale of silly chance.

Remember when purple crashed with green?
The fashion claims it's quite the scene!
With orange flecks, like a sunset fun,
These colors know how to make us run.

Laughter and fabric weave a story,
A dress that's bold, yet never hoary.
"A clashing mess?" the critics might scoff,
But oh, how we giggle and peel it off!

So wear your colors, bright and loud,
Defy the rules, and join the crowd.
In every shade, let joy embrace,
Together, we create our own grace.

The Silken Pin

A silken pin with endless style,
Perched on a collar, oh so viral.
It twirls around, a cheeky sprite,
"Come poke me, dear! I'm quite polite!"

With every jab, it makes a claim,
A fashion choice, or just a game?
It lifts the spirits, tugs the soul,
All while playing its silly role.

A fuss and flutter in the night,
This pin suggests, "Please hold me tight!"
With a twist and turn, it lights the way,
Witty charm in everyday play.

So here it sits, with laughter spun,
An artifact of whimsy fun.
Just one pin can change a name,
To dashing flair and dancing fame!

Graceful Illuminations

In the glow of jest, the crystals flare,
Shimmering stories floating in air.
"Who's got the spotlight?" they ask with glee,
Lighting up rooms, as bright as can be!

Beaming bright, they joke and tease,
With glimmers soft, they dance with ease.
"Look at me flare in mundane places,
Turning yawns into joyful graces!"

Each sparkle a line, a clever quip,
A luminescent little trip.
As laughter echoes through the night,
These shiny tales make hearts feel light.

So raise your glass to shining flair,
To luminous gems that fill the air.
For in the world where humor plays,
Light is the jewel that always stays!

The Graceful Keepsake

In a drawer, it lay, so shy,
A lopsided gem, oh me, oh my!
Dusted off for a fancy dance,
A chicken finally took a chance.

With sequins bright and colors bold,
It sparkled like a pot of gold.
A wobbly pin, it danced with glee,
Embracing the chaos, oh so free!

Upon my coat, it twirled with flair,
People laughed; they stopped to stare.
"What is that?" they quipped in jest,
I smiled and said, "Just my best guest!"

Now each party, it steals the show,
A treasure from the depths below.
As guests arrive and raucous play,
That quirky pin brightens the day!

Elysian Adornment

A gem that sparkles, yet feels quite plain,
Like a cat in socks—what a strange gain!
People whisper—"Is that for real?"
As it flops and flares, it starts to squeal.

Attached to my coat, it swayed with grace,
A fly as my date; what a funny case!
Jokingly I waved, it bounced in delight,
Making everyone giggle, what a sight!

"Is that a bird?" an old man asked,
As I twirl around, my hands quite masked.
I simply smiled with baton in hand,
In the spotlight now, so unplanned!

At the end of the night, oh what a thrill,
That silly adornment gave time a chill.
From laughter and joy, it never does part,
This quirky bauble, a true work of art!

A Touch of Forgotten Elegance

In the attic, it once did lie,
A dainty piece, never shy.
I pulled it out—a dusty clout,
With memories wrapped, I had no doubt.

It hugs my lapel, oh what a show,
With jewels that shimmer and colors that glow.
A missed connection, oh how it laughs,
A date with nostalgia, oh what gaffes!

"Is that a relic?" a kid exclaimed,
"Well, if it is, then I'm quite famed!"
I danced around, and so did it,
With twirls and dips, I threw a fit!

As the evening waned, the pin shined bright,
A stretch of laughter, hearts took flight.
From closet's gloom to party's cheer,
It's the oddball charm that keeps us near!

The Memorable Pin

Oh, this pin, a curious thing,
Wobbling around, it loves to swing!
To gatherings grand, it made its way,
Proclaiming its presence with shades of gray.

It once sported diamonds; now it's a joke,
But update its story, and laughter's evoked.
"Is that haute couture or thrift store flair?"
With a wink of fashion, I didn't care!

Among the crowd, it steals the night,
Awkward yet charming, a dazzling sight.
With laughter, light, and a playful spin,
Who knew such joy could come from a pin?

A tale it tells wherever it goes,
Of embarrassing moments and funny woes.
In its gleam, we find pure delight,
A silly treasure—a star of the night!

Threads of Luminous Memory

In a closet full of fluff and flair,
Hides a sparkle, brave and rare.
Worn with pride and a silly grin,
Who would guess the chaos within?

A twirl here, a stumble there,
Each step feels more like a dare.
It catches light, a dazzling flash,
Oh dear, I hope I don't crash!

Grandma's giggle lingers near,
As I dance about without fear.
An heirloom's charm, ironic fate,
It's a laugh, not just ornate!

With every pin, a tale is spun,
Mismatched gems all look like fun.
This wardrobe full of jokes and charms,
Wraps me tight in zany arms.

The Adorned Heart

A quirky pin upon my chest,
Its shine demands a brighter quest.
The hearts and stars in jumbled bliss,
Reflect a life that's hard to miss.

With each new outfit, comes the chat,
'Oh look, a cat with a party hat!'
Adorned with laughter, I'm a show,
A giggle fest wherever I go.

Friends all tease, 'You're quite the sight!'
A beacon of laughs, sheer delight.
They ask if I'm a fashion king,
But it's just my brooch that makes me sing.

Oh how it twinkles, rather proud,
In a crowd where silliness is allowed.
A masterpiece of what we wear,
With humor stitched into the flair.

Songs of the Ornate Soul

In the mirror, I see my muse,
A brooch of odd, delightful hues.
It hums a tune of days gone by,
Winking at me, oh so spry!

Each little gem sings its own song,
Playful notes that just feel wrong.
'There's a pearl that's lost its way!'
But who cares when we dance and play?

My friends all clap during the show,
As I prance like a disco pro.
With every turn, a reset twist,
I wonder if I'll sprain my wrist!

So here's to baubles, loud and proud,
Stand tall and laugh, oh did I shout?
For in this laughter's sweet embrace,
We find our joy in every trace!

Radiance Encased in Metal

A doodad shiny on my coat,
Reflecting life, each laugh we wrote.
It jingles softly, every bumble,
In this parade of friendly fumbles.

'What's that thing?' they ask with glee,
'A squirrel's tail or just a whimsy?'
I proudly shrug and laugh out loud,
It's simply me, no need for shroud!

The colors clink, a magic charm,
A memory wrapped, it feels so warm.
Friends don't just love the glimmer bright,
But the stories told in silly light.

Let's raise a toast, let worries cease,
For in this glee, we find our peace.
With every chuckle, we let it glow,
For radiant gems make the best show!

Serenity Wrapped in Timelessness

In a pocket of silence, a giggle breaks free,
Time stood still, with a wink, you see.
A laughter tickles, like sunbeams in flight,
Chasing the shadows, so silly, so bright.

A dance on the edge of a playful old clock,
Whispers of joy in the tick-tock rock.
With each silly moment, the mundane's outpaced,
Serenity bursts with a wink, and a grace.

An umbrella of joy, we open with flair,
Dancing in puddles, not worried about hair.
We twirl through the gossip of life's little tease,
Finding such sweetness in nonsense with ease.

With quirky old hat and mismatched old shoes,
We strut down the lane, making our own dues.
In the tapestry woven, so lively, distinct,
Lies a charm of the heart, in the laughter we linked.

Tapestry of Grace

A cat in a hat starts to prance down the lane,
Stealing old thimbles, not caring for fame.
With a flip and a twirl, there's a jingle of fun,
Creating a ruckus till day is done.

The spoons dance in rhythm, a clatter and clink,
A teapot's on fire, but it's all just a wink.
Colors are splattered, like paint on a spree,
As chaos and laughter embrace you and me.

A patchwork of smiles, oh, lively delight,
A circus of wonders, oh, what a sight!
With each little quirk, we craft tales anew,
In this canvas of giggles, there's room for the blue.

So grab a wild feather and lend me your cheer,
We'll dance through the mess, with nary a fear.
For in every mishap, there's beauty to trace,
And moments of joy, in this tapestry of grace.

The Secret Within the Setting

An old rocking chair creaks with a grin,
Holding the secrets of mischief within.
It knows about cupcakes and sneaky sweet pies,
And the way grandpa laughs as he gives you surprise.

A flowerpot winks, sprouting flowers in jig,
Swaying with breezes, a curious gig.
Each petal a whisper, a joke on its way,
Turning the mundane to bright sunny play.

Hidden in corners, a misfit of glee,
A sock with a smile and a tea bag with three.
The quirky old chair now leads us in song,
To dance where the silly truly belong.

So let's toast to the fun, the secret's unfurled,
With laughter and joy, let's twirl through the world.
For the simple is magic when you dress it in grace,
Finding chuckles and wonder in every odd place.

Flourish of Enchanted Gleam

In a garden of giggles, the daisies all bow,
As the wind whispers secrets to the curious cow.
Wobbling and bobbing, they sway to the breeze,
Adding a twinkle to moments with ease.

A playful old rabbit hops over to say,
"Do you want to join me in this merry display?"
The sun winks down, like it's part of the game,
While shadows throw capers, oh, isn't it sane?

With a splash of confetti and a twirl in the air,
All worries dissolve in this magical fair.
Each petal a giggle, a riotous dream,
In the dance of the flowers, we flourish, it seems.

Laughter's the sparkle, the heart of the scene,
Gems of hilarity, bright, bold, and keen.
As we bask in the glow of enchantment so bright,
Let's cherish the moment, with joy, pure delight!

The Treasure of Timeless Moments

In a field of daisies, I tripped with glee,
My shoe flew off, oh what a sight to see!
The sun laughed brightly, a cheeky old friend,
Said, 'Don't worry, dear, it's just a fashion trend.'

Each moment's a treasure, each laugh a delight,
I danced through the mishaps, oh what a night!
With friends all around, we collected the cheer,
A necklace of giggles, our memories here.

Captured in Glint

A shiny bauble caught my eye,
I thought it a charm, oh my, oh my!
But it was a bottle cap, twisted and neat,
Glistening proudly, what a treat!

We laughed and pretended it brought us good luck,
Magical moments, who needs a truck?
For in every sparkle lies a story to tell,
Of youthful folly and laughter's sweet spell.

Whispering Grace

In a garden of puns, we planted our dreams,
With flowers that giggle and giggles that beam.
A butterfly fluttered, it made such a buzz,
Telling all secrets, just because!

We danced in the sunshine, with hats full of flair,
Each flop and each tumble, we'd never compare.
Beneath the blue sky, we spun tales like gales,
Grace is a laugh that eternally sails.

The Gem of Inner Light

A gem beyond compare, so bright and so bold,
But check the tag, it's plastic, now sold!
Yet in our hearts, it shines like the sun,
Funny how laughter is the best kind of fun.

We strutted our stuff with our gems on display,
Chasing sparkles in life, come what may.
For jokes are the jewels that twinkle so clear,
In the treasure of laughter, we hold it so dear.

Legacy of Charm

A shiny pin upon my coat,
It said, 'I'm here, let's take a vote!'
With charms that giggle, sparkle, shine,
It caught the eye, oh how divine!

A dragonfly that rides the breeze,
A ladybug that makes you sneeze.
With colors bright and laughs galore,
This charm's the life, who could want more?

It winks, it nods, it tells a tale,
Of fashion faux pas that can prevail.
In pins and badges, let us boast,
Of all the laughter, we love most!

So wear your charms and strike a pose,
With friends around, anything goes!
In legacy of charm we find,
A joyous touch to humor bind!

Serene Adornment

Upon my chest, a badge of glee,
It twinkles bright, just wait and see!
With whispers soft, it tells a joke,
That leaves you chuckling till you choke!

A playful spin on fashion's face,
This piece brings joy, a funny grace.
With gemstones laughing, side by side,
Each glint a grin, oh what a ride!

A necklace here, a ribbon there,
Decorations that dare to share.
They tease and tickle, make us smile,
A funny story, every mile!

So take your gems and let them shine,
Each silly clip is yours and mine.
With serene adornments, here we stay,
To laugh and relish every day!

Whispers of Elegance

With whispers low, they tease and play,
These shiny bits that say hooray!
A flourish here, a wink or two,
They've got a story just for you!

A feathered friend, a playful catch,
It's hard to be serious, how can we match?
In elegance cloaked with humor's dress,
They laugh aloud, who could guess?

Each sparkle carries whispers bold,
Of secrets shared and tales retold.
In whimsy wrapped, I strut my best,
With joy as crown, I'm ever blessed!

So when in doubt, just pin it down,
A playful jest can flip the frown.
In whispers that dance, we'll navigate,
A world of charm that won't await!

The Jewel of Serenity

In quiet glee, my pin does shine,
A gem that plays with joy divine.
A quirky twist, a smile's embrace,
In every line, it finds its place.

A wink, a nod, it dances proud,
Among the chaos, it stands out loud.
With every sparkle, laughter flows,
A jewel that tickles, who knows?

As friends gather, it sparks delight,
Creating scenes both sweet and bright.
In gentle humor, we find our way,
With every laugh, come what may!

So let it shine, this gem of cheer,
In each moment, hold it dear.
The jewel of calm will always soar,
Through giggles shared, forevermore!

www.ingramcontent.com/pod-product-compliance
Lightning Source LLC
Chambersburg PA
CBHW070323120526
44590CB00017B/2802